Joe

Best Wishes

WHAT THEY WANTED

•

Victor Henry

Victor Henry

FUTURECYCLE PRESS

www.futurecycle.org

Published by FutureCycle Press
Lexington, Kentucky, USA

ISBN 978-1-942371-13-7

*In memory of my loving mother who worried and suffered immeasurably
the one year and twenty-seven days I was in Vietnam.*

CONTENTS

DRAFT NOTICE

3 May 1966

Late afternoon. Friday.
Sacramento simmers in hundred-degree heat.
Mom greets me, grim news in her voice,
A sorrow I'd heard a couple months before
At my father's funeral: the somber sadness
From which she'd never recovered.
For those fleeting mercurial moments
Between life and beyond,
I'd held Dad in my arms,
Heard his death rattle,
A staccato low-pitched gurgling sound,
Rode in the ambulance,
Called a Catholic priest,
Dealt with the nightmare.
I hear the faint sound
Of war drums beating,
Imagine my mother sobbing
Beside her son's coffin.
The fire and smoke of my life
Rise higher and higher.
My fate, a booby trap, detonates,
Destroys what's left of my fragile world.

THE NEW ENEMY

You had never met a Vietnamese
Until you went to Vietnam
In 1967, the Year of the Sheep.

Basic training
Taught you to kill
The new enemy.

Democracy and Freedom
Kept vigil every July 4th
As a reminder of past wars.

None of your high school teachers
Told you thousands of Vietnamese
Were shipped to France in 1939,

Used as cannon fodder
In the fight against Hitler.
Years later you discover

That the war was based on a lie.
That the Gulf of Tonkin incident
On August 4th never happened.

That Admiral James Stockdale
Flew air cover that night
For the Maddox and the C. Turner Joy.

That Stockdale realized
Washington was going to launch a war
Under false pretenses.

And much like Coleridge's *Ancient Mariner*
You, too, have the strange power of speech,
A tale to tell, to teach the man who must hear.

HOMETOWN HERO

Like a hometown hero from the heartland,
A poor black from the projects,
A son expected to emulate his father,
I'm drafted, wander off to war,
Told to kill for an idea,
To *Kill a Commie for Christ.*
My coworkers at the aircraft plant,
Both World War II and Korean veterans,
Agree, it's my patriotic duty, right or wrong,
To defend the flag, motherhood, the American Way.
It's understood we must bomb
North Vietnam back to the Stone Age.
That I must do my job, fight like a man.
In this Theatre of the Absurd,
I'm ordered to wage cruel war
On my own species in a country
That has never known peace.
Sheep-like, I never question my role.

OAKLAND ARMY INDUCTION CENTER

Terrified and dazed,
We stand with our toes flat
Against a yellow line
That separates us from them,
Four military doctors in white coats
From each branch of the service,
Yelling like tough guys
For us to bend over and spread our cheeks.
I look to my right and left,
Seeing young men with both hands
Clutching the fleshy part of their face.
They just don't get it.
We're all hemorrhoids here anyway.

WEAPONS CACHE

We've traveled on a military bus
From the Oakland Army Induction Center
To Fort Ord.

After piling off,
A corporal, wearing starched fatigues,
Spit-shined brogans, and a helmet liner,

Orders us to form five lines of ten men each,
To stand at attention,
To not move a muscle or make a sound.

He barks out commands
To dump our overnight bags
Onto the ground,

To put any weapons we have
In the plastic buckets
Being passed like collection plates.

From the back row
I see guys toss stilettos,
Saturday night specials,

Brass knuckles, blackjacks,
Ice picks, and other paraphernalia
Into the wire-handled canisters.

I hear metal strike metal,
Harsh discordant sounds
That grow heavier and heavier

As the bucket comes closer.
Only the guy next to me
Sees my contribution

Thrown into the brim-filled five-gallon container,
A tiny penknife Dad
Gave me as a graduation present

I use occasionally to pare my nails.

CANDY ASSES

During basic training,
Fort Riley, Kansas,
Was the asshole of the earth.

He spent nights
Crying in the latrine, beaten down,
Whimpering, mewling.

The other recruits
Thought he would wash out,
Be on the streets again, a free man.

But when he became a squad leader
In a strac killer platoon,
They depended upon him.

Especially the mama's boy,
A shit-bird, whose weapon always jammed
During a fire fight.

PRIVATE NUMNUTS

"Before we can get to a place of peace, we have to touch our suffering— embrace it and hold it." **At Hell's Gate: A Soldiers Journey from War to Peace** *(Claude Anshin Thomas)*

The Drill Instructor, veins protruding from his neck, yells at a platoon of new recruits to answer post haste. He says, "Which is easier to kill? A fly? Or," pointing to a recruit in the first row, "Private Numnuts over there?" With his left hand rolled tightly in a fist and the other with forefinger extended, he signals to Private Numnuts to move front and center. The platoon hears the whirring. The fly trapped inside the D.I.'s hand going bonkers. And, as quick as a gambler moving thimbles in a shell game, he has Private Numnuts by the throat. "Which is easier to kill?" He screams again to the platoon, standing at attention, outside on a very hot Kansas afternoon, sweating bullets in their skivvies. "The fly or Numnuts?" Paralyzed with fear, they are speechless, their mouths open, forming perfect round Os. "Numnuts!" he yells. "Goddammit! It's Numnuts!" The D.I. squeezes tighter and tighter until Private Numnut's eyes pop from their sockets. Now, speaking softly, almost in ecstasy, the D.I. slowly punctuates each word, saying, as innocently as a murderer confessing his sins, "Believe me, girls, I wouldn't hurt a fly."

UNCLE HERB

People visiting our 1940s house
Near the railroad tracks
On the east side of town
For the first time
See the photograph
Of Uncle Herb
In a boxer's stance.
Ft. Riley
Monogrammed on his trunks.
Because we look alike,
Twins perhaps,
They think it's a photograph of me.

Mother chokes up slightly,
Gets misty-eyed,
Chronicles the story of her younger brother,
A sergeant in the 194th Tank Battalion.
Captured in the Philippines.
Survived the POW camps,
The Bataan Death March,
Only to lose his life on the Arisan Maru,
A Japanese Hell Ship.

Sunk by the Shark,
An American submarine,
October 24th, 1944,
In the South China Sea.
Over 1800 POWs sent to Japan
As slave labor.

Our family revered Uncle Herb,
The war hero.
When my turn came to protect our country,
To fight for democracy,
To combat communism,
I willingly went to Vietnam.

One cold, nasty night in December,
During advanced unit training,
I phone from Custer Hill.

"Mother," I say, "Herb trained here."
Was quartered at Custer Hill.
Was in a mechanized infantry unit as well.

Fear, a foreign soldier,
Flows from my lips
Like a glacier.
She reassures me
Nothing terrible will happen.
And in her words,
Suspended between speech and silence,
I hear Uncle Herb's voice.

FIRST LOVE

For over twenty days
You've been topside
On a ship headed for Vietnam.
You're nineteen and naive.

She'd sent you a Dear John letter
During basic training.
Yet you still love her.
In the Fall semester

She'd asked you out for a date.
Three months later,
After proposing marriage,
You dropped out of school,

Got drafted.
At the drive-in that spring,
You kissed her,
Named your children.

You look over the side of the ship,
See white water
Cutting across the bow
Like a cloud being separated

By a strong wind.
You think of her often,
Feel like dying,
Jumping overboard.

You float farther and farther
From her as if you're being pulled
By a current with a logic of its own.
In her last letter she confessed

She'd found someone else.
Now pinned down under fire,
In the mud and the rain,
You're so close

To the earth you swear
You can smell

The fragrance of her hair,
Smell her perfume,

Smell the sweet scent
Of her sex,
Feel her soft skin.
When RPG rounds and mortars

Pound your perimeter
You scream hard for your mother.

JUMPING SHIP

That morning at chow
Rumors float like jettisoned debris.
Psycho Man leaped over the railing
Sometime after midnight
On the way to the ship's brig,
Handcuffs straining against
Blood and bone,
Plunging feet first

Into the cold, black sea.
Each time one of the MPs
Threw him a life preserver,
He pushed it away.
For a few minutes
He was in the spotlight,
Bobbing up and down
Like an unsinkable cork

Before being sucked
Into the ship's propellers.
That afternoon, while searching
In circles for the P Man,
We listen to Hanoi Hannah
On a shortwave receiver.
She knows we're coming,
Knows our troop strength,

Knows the names of our officers,
Predicts how many of us will die
In the coming year.
Later, like derelicts huddled
Around a bonfire, we listen to
The Lakers play Philadelphia
From the Sports Arena,
Jerry and Elgin

Against Hal and Wilt,
A game we understand.

LIBERATION

He was there to liberate
The oppressed of South Vietnam.
But when his convoy drove up Highway One
To Camp Bearcat,
All he saw were American soldiers,
Standing or lying by the side of the road,
As if the war zone he had been prepared for
Was in another country.
"Where's the war?" he asked his friend
Sitting next to him.
Stopping at a checkpoint
Near a hamlet,
His friend pointed to an old woman,
Staring intensely at them with hatred.
"There," he said, "In her eyes."

CAR WASH

That sweltering April summer afternoon
When Ramirez and I take a 5-ton
Down to the river
To wash the red dirt
From its banged-up olive drab body,
I leave my M-16 inside the cab,
Propped against the sandbagged floorboard,
Concealed from children
Playing in the tepid water nearby.
I enter a crude dwelling
Lacking electricity and plumbing.
Smell the paraffin odor from a candle stub
On a saucer in the center of the table.
See the hole underneath the bed
Surrounded by the dirt floor.
A faded photo of Father Ho
Tacked upon the wall
Of the dimly lit hut
Looks down at us.
Together the old ones
Pour green tea
Into a cracked bowl,
Their fingers like frail fans
Opening and closing.
I recognize sadness
In the old woman's face.
See my mother
At the airport
For the last time
Before flying back to Ft. Riley,
My right arm holding her shoulder
As if she's the child,
Her mouth downturned,
Her heart broken.

WHITE MICE

We're in a convoy
Stopped at a narrow bridge
While two MPs and a couple
Of South Vietnamese Police

Argue and gesture. The White Mice
Are on one side , the MPs on the other.
I see one of the White Mice
Motion for a deuce-and-a-half

Towing two trailers of ammo,
Filled full of mess equipment,
And two cooks, to cross the bridge.
Everything happens in slow motion

As if it has been orchestrated
And this is the final take.
The Six-By slides into a rice paddy,
Turns over from the weight

Of the ammo trailers.
What looks like no more
Than two to three feet of water
Must seem like an ocean

To those trapped.
The driver emerges
A couple of minutes later,
Gasping for breath.

I don't see the cooks.
Disbelief turns to anger.
I curse the White Mice's incompetency.
Two cooks drown in a ditch

While black-clad peasant women
In conical straw hats
Replant green seedlings.

UNFRIENDLIES

We've had easy duty
All morning long
Protecting an engineering unit
Searching for mines
On a dirt road
Near Xuan Loc
Before the rest
Of the convoy advances.

We've lit 'em up.
Lucky Strikes, Pell Mells, Kents.
Smoked 'em down
To the brown stains
On our fingers.
Won a major pissing contest
That'll be talked about
In both base camps
For the duration of the war.

Bet a dozen cases
Of beer that their boy
Would uncover a mine
So explosive
It would make a howitzer
Sound like a toe popper.

While we're chowing
Down on our Cs,
Wesley, the bear,
Spots five or six Viet Cong
Moving through the underbrush
Like a small herd of gazelles.

An engineer
Hands me
A pair of field glasses.
I watch Charles
Stepping lightly,
Rushing to meet us
In a confrontation
We'll write home about.

I see their pockmarked faces,
Witness one of them grimacing,
His fingers tightly gripping
The carrying handle
Of the 60mm mortar.
Behind him, the number two man
Hauls the ammo.
The rest hold their AKs
In the ready position,
Metal and man welded together.

We call S-2, intelligence,
Expect instantaneous permission
To rain on their parade.
I feel the old adrenaline rush
Surging through my body,
Hear everyone locking and loading.

Instead, intelligence orders us
To vacate the premises.
Informs us
There are no unfriendlies here,
Convinces us we're seeing ghosts.

We look out into the jungle,
Watch moving shadows dissolve.

PERIMETER

We've filled sandbags all afternoon,
Setting up a perimeter
In a clear and secured area.

A couple of hours later,
During a hard monsoon rain,
We're ordered to slit the bloated bags

With bayonets and move camp
300 meters north before night falls.
Wet, exhausted, pissed off,

Some of us slip into slumberland,
Dream of family, friends, freeways.
The rest of us curse

The 5th VC Infantry Division
For not showing up to the party.
Asleep in a Vietnamese graveyard,

Danny calls out for Lan,
His girlfriend, a dancer at the Pagoda Club.
In the half light of the morning,

A couple of us see a black scorpion
Scamper across the wet red dirt,
Plant a perverted hicky on his neck,

A kiss so provocative,
Danny moans for more.

AWOL

Riding from Stockton to Oakland to Ft. Ord,
We reminisce about our high school days,
Laugh because we never fit in.
He's from Stockton; I'm from Lodi.
Swear on a pint of sloe gin
We'd dated some of the same girls.

We're unsure what this war is all about,
Can't figure out why
We're fighting people halfway around the world.
We're draftees.

At Ft. Ord we talk one more time
Before I'm shipped to Fort Riley, Kansas.
Eight months later we meet again in Tay Ninh.
I'm outa here in four months and a wake up, I say.

He confesses this is his first day in Vietnam,
That he went AWOL.
Reveals to me he missed his family, his girl too much.
Informs me the Military Police hunted him,
Interrogated his parents, dogged his girlfriend,
Cross-examined his former employer.

Finally, after living underground for eight months,
He turned himself in.
The army, he says, gave him a choice:
Vietnam or Leavenworth.

Now, nearly three decades later,
I recall the day we met in Tay Ninh for the last time,
Puffs of smoke appearing and disappearing
On the Black Virgin Mountain behind us
Like phantoms in tulle fog.

Hear him confess to me, venom in his voice,
That this war is a curse that will follow us to our graves.

FLAK JACKET

Sometimes when it was too hot
To wear a shirt
And Major Stiles wasn't around
Handing out Article 15s
Like they were all-purpose capsules,
Bobby Joe wore his flak jacket
Unzipped,
Flaunted his white belly
And farmer's tan,
Risked the demotion
And loss of pay.

His bro, Stevie R,
Liked to strip to his waist.
Showed off his 18-inch biceps.
Boasted he'd gotten his guns
At Al's Gym in Jersey.

Three Rivers, a Hopi Indian,
Felt like a buffalo hunter
Wrapped in a wool overcoat
During the dead of summer.
He'd sprinkle the ground
With red dirt to cover the red
Of his spirit
In this part of Indian country.

Bobbie Joe, Stevie R, and Three Rivers
Cleaned their M-16s
On top of the track.
Sat cross-legged
Like tribal chiefs at a powwow,
Drank warm Kool-Aid from their canteens.

It was so hot and humid
That vest and man bonded
Like peanut butter
Stuck to the roof of your mouth.

Last night
Bobby Joe dreamt
He'd met his wife
In Honolulu on R&R.

Stevie R ranted:
"It's him or me,
Kill or be killed."
Said, "Ain't this a bitch."
We hunt Charles for weeks,
And he don't want no part
Of our shit.

Now, worked up
Into a lather,
Stevie R slapped a clip
Into his M-16,
Chambered a round,
Flipped off the safety,
And pulled the trigger.

Bobby Joe groaned
Like someone hit him
In the solar plexus.
A crimson spot,
The size of a dime,
Appeared near his open flak jacket
Just above his heart.

He toppled over the side of the track,
Landed face down,
Sprawled and twisted
In the red dirt.

The only man Stevie R
Killed during his tour
In Vietnam.

DROOPY DAWG

He sits on his cot sharpening his killing knife,
A Bowie that can easily cut through metal, even steel.
Droopy Dawg, a self-appointed mercenary from Charlie Company,

Takes money for patrols.
He barks in a slow southern accent
That he kills gooks for a price.

He's an expert with an M-79 Grenade Launcher.
Tonight at Camp Bearcat, before we go out tomorrow morning,
Many of us are getting stoned, getting juiced,

Getting totally ripped.
It is 1967 and this shit is no longer fun.
Too many of us are ending up in *The Stars and Stripes,*

KIAs dead and going home!
Droopy volunteers to take a ride with the LRRPs
On their tracks into the bush.

He's got over $1500 on him stashed in a money belt
He had specially made in Saigon.
To some of us he's a real up-and-coming entrepreneur,

Claims he's going to start his own business
When he gets back to the world.
When the LRRPs come back the next day

I hear Droopy bought the farm, got zapped,
Got wasted.
That when he got to Graves Registration

All he had on him was an empty wallet,
His girlfriend's picture,
And a debt of death Uncle Sam could never repay.

DUST OFF

A medivac chopper flies
On a slant into a cold LZ
To pick up a Lt. Col,
Two Brigade majors
And three wounded grunts.

The dead brass lay
On ponchos
In the pouring rain,
Droplets streaming down
Their freshly shaven faces.

Three WIAs,
Scared and bleeding,
With stomach and leg wounds,
Beg for a ride out,
Pleading for a freedom bird

Like grunts near the end
Of their tour.
Men scramble to load the wounded
While the dust-off chopper
Sits shimmying and shaking.

The chopper pilot
Waves them off,
Points to the KIAs,
The index finger of his flight glove
Swaggering like a short-timer's stick.

THE BOOT

What could he have been thinking
When those 155mm howitzer shells
Came in on top of him?
How deep did he burrow into the ground?
Did he bitch while his breath was being sucked from his lungs?
Did he scream over and over again for his artillery support
To stop the death drain?

Today we are gathered in a stand-down.
Men have died because a captain from Bravo Company
Miscalculated his fire mission.
Short rounds fell short of their target.
Like Vietnamese civilians caught in a crossfire
Of instantaneous death,
He must have felt what it was like to *di-di mau*
In the face of fire.

Only a few of us have seen the boot,
Shattered broken bone, soft flesh, coagulated blood,
Stump protruding from its casing, identifiable as a left foot.
I notice the leather toe is scuffed beyond a spit shine.
I see the olive drab fabric worn through in spots,
Small holes burrowing through into festering flesh.
The olive drab sock, burnt and frayed around the edges,
Sticks to the tissue like napalm.

The boot sits in front of me like an icon,
A symbol, a prop in a one act play.
I study it, touch it, pick it up, talk to it.
I knew the whole part.
I give in to war's insanity,
Admit this war has reduced the living
And those other men, those dead men, to body parts.

R & R

All the bars in Yokohama
Look the same. For over two hours
You've been nursing beers

In the dim light of Washington Square,
Its interior dark like dusk,
Trying to forget Vietnam,

Trying to forget your girl
Who has forgotten you,
Drowning your sorrows,

Feeling a sinful strain of unbearable shame,
Numbing your broken heart
Like a man freezing to death in a cold sea.

At this time, you are farther from home
Than you've ever been before.
You scrawl FTA on the moist table,

Then casually watch tiny rivulets
Inch their way to the edge
Like a curtain of water falling over a dam.

Later, downstairs, in the John,
An American G.I. in civvies
Butts his head against a white porcelain stall,

Repeating over and over again:
"I'm a marine, I'm a marine,"
Blood flowing from his forehead.

When she sits next to you,
You're so far into a back-home reverie
You don't even know she's there.

She speaks fluent English,
Buys you another beer,
Asks you to dance.

She senses your innocence,
Knows you've been with only a few women,
Offers her body as home.

Later she teaches you how to please a woman,
Transposes pleasure for pain.

CHILLS AND FEVER

Benny Mays and I were fed up with jungle warfare and our tour in Vietnam. So Benny, a young black man from Watts, refused to go on a night patrol. He'd had a vision, warning him that night's combat assault would not be a bargain of events. The next morning a kangaroo court was held. A rear echelon officer addressed the jury. "We have not been training Barbie dolls to kill Viet Cong," he screamed. "This soldier disobeyed an order." The lieutenant assumed the air of a mythical god, delighting in a perverse passion for justice, and delivered his Pied Piper offering like the last of the true believers. His voice echoed throughout the courtroom as if each word was a blow from the axe wielder. Benny, suffering chills and fever, sagged to his knees like a sunken fence.

BENEATH A THIN LAYER OF LIFE

Tet 1968

Incoming mail arrives,
A barrage in the black hours of the night,
Messianic visitors from space.
Meteoritic showers of mortar rounds,
Defying darkness,
Penetrate the perimeter,
Malignant in execution.
Our new point man takes a direct hit,
A lob shot
Landing on top of his steel pot.
He vanishes.
At the entrance of a corrugated iron bunker,
A buddy lies frozen in the fetal position.
Beneath a thin layer of life,
He ruminates about the progeny of permanence
As Viet Cong,
Overseeing death and destruction,
Infiltrate the landscape like ghosts.

BUDDY SYSTEM

Frank calls today,
Says The Buzzard
Checked out from a drug overdose.
I ask if Tony, Wild Bill Ramirez,
Odom and Nichols know.
That's all that's left of us now.
We congratulate each other
For surviving the Nam, so far.
Who would have guessed
Sutton would die of AIDS two years ago
While directing a production of *Strange Snow*.
Who would have guessed Max
Would drink himself to death,
Survive three marriages,
Bear a child born without a brain,
Another born with web feet,
Lose more jobs than a company
Downsizing in the middle of the night?
Who would have believed Nate Longley
Would be killed in a freak accident,
A beam giving way
On a high-rise 55 stories up?
Turner was predictable.
When he held up that branch
Of Bank of America and was obliterated
By the swat team, we weren't too surprised.
"Yeah," Frank says, "Life's a goddamn S & D mission."
You come back from getting your ass kicked
in an ambush and years later
You still dwell on the things
That were significant then.
How you would have done the mission differently.
Now, forty years later, after normalization,
You go back to Vietnam on company business,
Help establish a capitalistic base
In what once was a communist stronghold.
"Frank," I ask, "What the hell was that war all about?"

THE DIOXIN BLUES

An unemployed Vietnam veteran in his late forties requests a physical examination at an army hospital. He has discovered a group of tumors near his rib cage, each tumor no larger than a button. For the past five months he has had a mysterious pulmonary condition, a pulmonary condition so severe he's cracked a rib from coughing, unsuccessfully diagnosed recently by two private doctors. A half an hour later, a nurse draws a sample of his blood. While the syringe fills, he recalls a sweltering afternoon when his recon platoon had stopped for a ten-minute rest, tracking VC on a crossroad of the Ho Chi Minh Trail. He removed his flak vest and trudged mechanically toward a dying flower, inspecting it like a botanist studying an unidentified specimen. Its petals hung lifelessly like loose wires attached to the arms of a jointed puppet. Near the weakened flower, a People Sniffer registered his body odor, its metal snout saturated with Agent Orange. Earlier that morning he had seen low-flying aircraft upwind in his area administering an aerosol attack, engulfing the surrounding area in a mist of fog. Now he looks morosely into the nurse's eyes. He tries to tell her this arm belongs to a VC, an NVA, a Vietnamese peasant. Faltering, he asks if he can take a smoke break. Moments before the black hood of death is lowered over his head.

JIMMY LEE

Jimmy Lee jacks up
The front wheel
Of Babe the Blue Ox,
My 1964 Buick LeSabre,
And removes it
Like a pit crew mechanic
At the Indy Five Hundred.

Afterwards he chugalugs
Another cold Miller Lite
In what must be
Record-breaking time.
I love him like a brother,
This Irish misfit,
Long red hair

Flowing past his shoulder blades
Like a Viking warlord.
Before tackling the serious stuff,
We've inhaled two 12-packs
While watching the 49ers play
The Rams to a 35-35 tie.
Laughing deeply from lungs

Already donated
To Johns Hopkins,
Jimmy Lee tells the clerk
At Safeway
I'm this week's $1000 winner
In their football contest.
It's five in the afternoon;

A typical sweltering summer sun
Blisters the concrete patio floor
Of my San Joaquin Valley villa.
Hot enough to fry quesadillas
On the cement.
Jimmy Lee has descended
from the Sierra Nevadas

Like a trapper on the take
To fix The Ox,
Loving her like

She's his better half.
We're both students
At the local state university,
Vietnam veterans

Living on the G.I. Bill.
Jimmy Lee sleeps in a trailer
Amongst the pines in thin air.
I rent a cottage that has no heat
Or central air in the barrio
On the west side of town.
We're both social pariahs,

A couple of modern-day misfits.
We don't care about anyone or anything,
Dead men in our own homecoming parade
Carrying each other's coffins.
The socket slips from his hold,
Falls fast from his fingertips,
Knuckles scraping hard against metal,

Blood instantly appearing like sunspots.
For less than a welcome-home hug
Or one more reminder we lost the war,
Jimmy Lee swears he'll get The Ox
On the road again within the hour,
Then drains the last drop
Of foam from another dead soldier,

Crumples it in his hand.
He bets me
Before the next cold one
Touches the sides
He'll have replaced
The ball bearings,
Bled the breaks,

Changed the oil,
And tuned her up.
Since he came back
From Vietnam
He rarely talks
About the war,
Only of sin and forgiveness.

G.I. PARTY

For D. M., Vietnam veteran—
Committed suicide—1984

Today you reached retirement
With a disturbed and primal conscience.
Two 12-gauge Remington shotgun shells
Saturated the field of ice
That separated body count
From catatonic commitment.
Drunk and stoned,
Down in your worst moment,
You subpoenaed yourself
Into believing
The mission
Was more important
Than the man.

A CIVIL WAR FOR YOUR SOUL

You keep asking the same question
Over and over again
To those who will not listen:
If it wasn't a civil war,
Then why were we fighting
Men, women, and children?

Like Kerouac on the road,
A hobo riding the rails,
A saint in search of the Grail,
You separate reality from fantasy,
Select Fellini as your point man,
Cross over life's invisible line of demarcation
And remove your Rosencrantz and Guildenstern doubt.

For years you've looked for Vietnam
After Vietnam
In the drugs you took,
In the alcohol you consumed,
Until you saw the Big Lie for what it was.

Now you know how lemmings feel
Going over the cliff,
Know how pigs and cattle feel
When they're led down the chute,
Know how young men feel
When they're cannon fodder
In another senseless war.

Left alone like a refugee
Forced to choose between two countries,
You stave off sadness and suicide,
Contesting your demons,
In a civil war for your soul.

AFTER THE FALL

When Saigon fell in April 1975, you were in Australia
Waiting for the winning numbers in the Opera House lottery,
Expatriated from your family, from your friends, from your country.

For seven years you self-exiled yourself from the U.S.
Then, like a man recently released from prison,
You returned home to California, a foreigner, a newcomer, a visitor.

You enrolled in a community college, took an American history class,
Learned from the past what mistakes will be made again in the future.
Began reading the history of Vietnam, starting with the *1954 Geneva Accords*

And *The Pentagon Papers*. You replaced willful ignorance with critical thinking,
Examined the moral imperatives leading to the war,
Questioned the unnecessary deaths of three- to five-million
Brown-skinned people in Laos, Cambodia, and Vietnam.

Declared you'd never trust the government again, never trust politicians again.
You scorned warmongers and war profiteers. But those you despise the most
Are the pseudo patriots, those who use patriotism to silence criticism against

Those holding them in contempt.

WHAT THEY WANTED

Was my soul, my body, my mind.
Instead, what they got
Was a declaration to wage war on the war.

In the Nam,
During my relationship
Between being the manipulated
And the manipulator,
I was nothing more
Than U.S. Grade "A" American meat,
Used for some bureaucrat's political gain.

Now, over forty years later,
In this war of no fronts,
An MIA in my own country,
I sleep lightly,
Keep a knife nearby on the night stand,
Continue to go on night patrols,
Look for an alternative revenge.

LOCAL BOARD NO. 32

During the Vietnam War two thirds who went enlisted

For years now I've longed for
The executive secretary, the principal clerk,
To understand that her decisions
Were the reasons why twelve men
From my hometown died in Vietnam.

That Congress had not formally declared war,
That there was no clear and present danger,
That there was no need to impose a draft,
That I need her to explain to me
Why I was drafted when others were not.

That her signature on my induction notice
Was like a death warrant.
Old matriarch and executioner,
You could have been anybody's mother or grandmother,
And I wondered then, as I do now,

How many of your sons and grandsons got drafted.
How many died in the red dirt and monsoon mud of Vietnam.

ACKNOWLEDGMENTS

The following poems, some in different versions, first appeared in the following publications:

Revenge and Forgiveness: An Anthology of Poems: "What They Wanted"

Slipstream: "The Dioxin Blues"

Nobody Gets Off the Bus: Viet Nam Generation Big Book: "G.I. Party," "Chills and Fever"

Viet Nam Generation: A Journal of Recent History and Contemporary Culture: "White Mice," "Buddy System," "Oakland Army Induction Center," "Beneath a Thin Layer of Life"

Vietnam War Poetry: "Local Board No. 32," "Candy Asses," "Dust Off," "Droopy Dawg," "The New Enemy," "First Love," "After the Fall," "Jimmy Lee," "Draft Notice," "Hometown Hero," "Weapons Cache," "Private Numnuts," "AWOL," "Jumping Ship," "Liberation," "Car Wash," "Perimeter," "Flak Jacket," "A Civil War of the Soul"

Cover photo of the author in South Vietnam (September 24, 1967); author photo by Jennifer Lagier; cover and interior book design by Diane Kistner; Legacy Sans text with Copperplate titling

ABOUT FUTURECYCLE PRESS

FutureCycle Press is dedicated to publishing lasting English-language poetry books, chapbooks, and anthologies in both print-on-demand and ebook formats. Founded in 2007 by long-time independent editor/publishers and partners Diane Kistner and Robert S. King, the press incorporated as a nonprofit in 2012. A number of our editors are distinguished poets and writers in their own right, and we have been actively involved in the small press movement going back to the early seventies.

The FutureCycle Poetry Book Prize and honorarium is awarded annually for the best full-length volume of poetry we publish in a calendar year. Introduced in 2013, our Good Works projects are anthologies devoted to issues of universal significance, with all proceeds donated to a related worthy cause. Our Selected Poems series highlights contemporary poets with a substantial body of work to their credit; with this series we strive to resurrect work that has had limited distribution and is now out of print.

We are dedicated to giving all of the authors we publish the care their work deserves, making our catalog of titles the most diverse and distinguished it can be, and paying forward any earnings to fund more great books.

We've learned a few things about independent publishing over the years. We've also evolved a unique, resilient publishing model that allows us to focus mainly on vetting and preserving for posterity the most books of exceptional quality without becoming overwhelmed with bookkeeping and mailing, fund-raising activities, or taxing editorial and production "bubbles." To find out more about what we are doing, come see us at www.futurecycle.org.

Made in the USA
San Bernardino, CA
04 February 2016